THE SECRET OF
ABRAHAM

Tokunbo Emmanuel

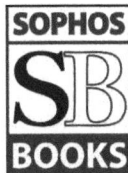

SOPHOS
SB
BOOKS

Raising the voice of Wisdom!

The Secret of Abraham
Copyright © 2006 by Tokunbo Emmanuel
Reprinted 2012
Revised 2017

Published by
SOPHOS Books
163 Warbank Crescent
Croydon
United Kingdom
CR0 0AZ

ISBN 978-1-905669-83-7

Cover design by *Maestro Creativity*
Printed in the Federal Republic of Nigeria

CONTENTS

To the wife of my youth, Linda,

and the fruit of our union,

Destiny, Daniel and David.

ACKNOWLEDGEMENTS

No great achievement is attributable to a single person. Many great people, in one way or another, have helped to make this work possible. This extremely partial list is in no way exhaustive.

I am thankful to Dr. Hugh Osgood for his fatherly support, leadership and wisdom. Pastor Sunday Adelaja's ministry and message are exemplary. I appreciate the impact he has made in my life to date.

Thanks to Seyi Ajayi for his continued interest in the progress of my life's mission. A special thanks to everyone at *Cornerstone Christian Centre* where I first shared this message in part.

Many thanks to my mum, Pastor Esther Olulaja for her prayers; to Rev. Ola Kris & FT for their refreshing friendship, and to all the members of *Paradise Christian Centre.*

Special thanks to Bishop Olaleye for his encouragement and generosity, and to my friends and partners around the world.

I have been blessed by the creativity of Michael Masade Jr., my graphic designer on the Well-digger Trilogy.

I could not have accomplished anything without the support of my dear wife, Linda, and great children, Destiny, Daniel and David. Thank you for allowing me time to pray and write. I love you all from my heart.

Finally, my God and Father, ever faithful and true; He alone deserves the highest praise for transforming my approach to life and ministry with His revelation and Truth.

- Tokunbo Emmanuel

Books With A Mission

FOREWORD

I am very impressed by the book that Pastor Emmanuel has written. Personally, I regard him highly as one of the most gifted Christian writers of our time. His books are not mere knowledge, but true revelations. *The Secret of Abraham* will open up your cities and nations for you to take them over for God.

In my personal ministry, this particular *secret* has been a major key to the breakthroughs we have experienced in Ukraine. I encourage you not just to read this first piece of the trilogy; be sure to read the whole series that Pastor Emmanuel is proposing to us.

However, beyond reading, take up the responsibility to become a deliverer and world-changer of your generation.

Sunday Adelaja

Senior Pastor, The Embassy of God Church, Kyiv, Ukraine.

INTRODUCTION

The story of Abraham has been told and retold countless times over the ages. Not only did the man Abram, who later became Abraham, become central to God's plan of salvation, the culmination of which is in Christ, his walk of faith is worthy of emulation. There is so much to learn from his sojourn on earth.

We who live in the dispensation of Grace need to pay particular attention to the numerous lessons from Abraham's life because he preceded the Law and knew God on the basis of promise. Even God encourages us to *"look to Abraham"* and gain understanding. *"When I called him,"* God said, *"he was but one, and I blessed him and made him many."* (Isaiah 51:2).

11

By "looking" at this elder of the faith, we begin to understand the dynamics of *our* walk of faith and how to fully appropriate the privilege of knowing God.

One of God's desires for choosing us is fruitfulness. He chose you and I *"to go and bear fruit - fruit that will last."* (John 15:16). By considering the life of Abraham, we can gain valuable insight into how our lives can bear fruit for God.

My intention in this book is not to highlight all the lessons from Abraham's life. Other commentaries have done a comprehensive job of this. However, there is *a particular secret* that is not common knowledge, a secret we cannot afford *not* to know. This secret will revolutionise the life of anyone who discovers it. Abraham would not have inherited the promises of God without the application of *this secret*. His achievements and influence would have been short-lived if he did not employ the strategy you are about to unveil. Once you discover and understand it, I am certain, your life will no longer remain the same. This *secret* will transform everything about you.

We will start from the beginning of Abraham's life of faith and build up to this mystery of enduring legacies. Do not skip the pages in search of *the secret* as there are many valuable truths that give it context. Be sure to increase in understanding line upon line, precept upon precept.

As Abraham's story unfolds, customise your reading experience and make appropriate application. I have written in a way *"to stimulate you to wholesome thinking."* Be prepared to engage with wisdom and truth. You have been given space to write *your own* action points. As the light of wisdom shines within you, make notes of how you can *own* the insights. You owe yourself this duty; *you* must make this commitment for the sake of fulfilment.

The Secret of Abraham transcends generations and cultures. It applies to you today. In fact, everyone who has attained any kind of significance in this life found and adapted this secret.

Two other volumes will follow this one to complete the trilogy of wisdom. May you find *your* path to fulfilment as you journey alongside Abraham, the friend of God.

I have chosen to use "Abraham" throughout the book even when his name was still "Abram." Also, most references to "man," "he," "him," "his" etc. are generic, including both men and women.

1
HIGH CALLING

"The God of glory appeared to our father Abraham
while he was still in Mesopotamia, before he lived
in Haran. 'Leave your country and your people,'
God said, 'and go to the land I will show you.'"
(Acts 7:2,3)

T rue greatness starts with God. Abraham's did. Before God appeared to him, not much was known about the ex-Chaldean. Until a man discovers himself in God, anything else he might be or become has no eternal significance. Achievements and status that last will always be traced back to God. He is the origin of all creativity the source of all ingenuity. Without Him, nothing is made that was made. Abraham came to realise that he was *made* by God after he met with his Maker.

You do not *determine* your course in life; you *discover* it. The path of discovery begins with encountering the Almighty. Somehow, estranged man has to rediscover his Creator by revelation. Without revelation, there can be no self-discovery. Without self-discovery, there can be no direction in life. Without direction, there can be no sense of destiny. Without this awareness of destiny, lost man will spend a lifetime in search of *his* place in the earth. Man's ordained place is *in* God. Man's purpose is to life *for* God. Man's peace is *with* God. Until man finds God, there is little hope of lasting peace.

Abraham did not *find* God. God *found* him. God appeared to him while he was still a worshipper of other gods. This is Grace. Because man cannot reach up to the heights to locate God, the Almighty will reach down to the depths to find man. God broke through the barriers of idolatry and "appeared" to Abraham. This appearance was the beginning of Abraham's life - his new life.

When God "appears" to man, He speaks *words*. The *appearance* is not as important as the *utterance*. Some look for the *spectacular* and miss the *specific*. The still small voice, at times, carries more weight than the thunder, earthquake and fire put together. Why get excited by a vision of the night when the interpretation of the vision remains a mystery in the day? Certainly, Abraham was amazed by Elohim's presence. More than this, he was quickened by the Almighty's voice.

God's word to Abraham was the beginning of a divine relationship. It brought to life a keen sense of direction, purpose and calling. The encounter was impacting enough to uproot Abraham from the place of comfort and usher him towards the promise of greatness. From that moment of discovery, Abraham could not shake off the deep consciousness of God and the call that laid hold of him.

Those who easily divert their course at the face of adversity have not really discovered their call. High callings are matters of *conviction* and not *convenience*. Unfavourable circumstances can dissuade the half-hearted but not the person with a conviction.

Continuous exposure to God's voice increases conviction to the point of *identifi-*

cation. When a man fully identifies himself with his call, no sacrifice is too big for its pursuit. Abraham found in God the reason for his existence. He fully identified with his call and left the known for the unknown. He understood that the "unknown" was only unknown to him but not to the God who called him; the God who knows all things.

God will always communicate the *end* result of His call from the *beginning* (not necessarily the detail in-between). The joy of what lies ahead, thus revealed, motivates the called in times of uncertainty. Through God, this end is not only captivatingly glorious, it is also more real than any prevailing circumstance. The naked eye may not see *the end* but the eye of not only sees it, but focuses intently on it.

Provided there is a live access to the all-seeing God, it is possible and rewarding to navigate from darkness into light; from uncertainty towards certainty; from emptiness into fulfilment. This is what the call of Abraham entailed. Achieving the end of his call was more important than mere existence in Ur. God called Abraham for a divine end. God needed him to take a divine journey. Abraham had no choice but to obey because he discovered that for this reason came he into the world; for this reason was he Abraham.

Abraham was called to possess a *land* and produce a *people*. At the time of his calling, he owned no real estate and had no child of his own. What an impossible call for a barren man! But remember, God never calls the equipped. He *equips* the called. God is not looking for *ability*; His priority is *availability*. He does not call man to do the *possible*, but to believe in the God of *possibilities*. The One who calls is faithful and more than able to accomplish the purpose for which He calls the called.

Every high calling from God is a thousand times bigger than the called. Reduce it to size and it no longer resembles a divine call. Reintroduce God to the picture (open your eyes to His word again; "count the stars," like Abraham was ordered to do at a crucial point in his journey— see Genesis 15:5) and watch the dimensions of vision multiply many fold. From one man to a great nation. From one nation to all the families of the earth. That sounds like God to me!

The call may be massive, but it is not unattainable. The One who calls is committed to teaching the called everything he needs to succeed in his mission. Abraham had much to learn. God had much to teach. *The ability to learn from God is what guarantees arrival at the destination of ones call.* God's curricular of greatness is designed to increase man from within until he grows to fit the size of his high calling. If man cannot learn, he will not grow; and if man does not grow, he will not be fit for his destination. Generally, man is a slow learner; but thankfully, God is a patient Teacher. He found Abraham useable because Abraham was teachable.

Amongst many things, God taught Abraham the principles of faith. He also taught him *the secret of influence.* This secret was a major key to possessing the land of promise. *This secret is available to everyone who has been called as he was.*

The path of God's call is the place where God blesses. *"Leave your country,"* God said, *"and I will bless you."* If Abraham stayed in Ur, he would have missed the blessing. Countless people have forfeited the blessing because of the convenience of their present and prevailing circumstances. Present comfort, no matter how plentiful, cannot compare with the overflowing blessedness contained in the call of God. Moreover, every call from above opens the door of opportunity to *walk* and *work* closely with the Creator of the universe. Abraham embraced the privilege; he took the plunge and became a history-maker.

Over to You

Have you discovered your high calling in God? Have you heard His voice calling forth your destiny?

God calls everyone uniquely by name. You are not here by accident. You have not come to know God by chance. He has a custom-made purpose for your life here on earth.

Do not brush God aside. Do not close your ears when He calls. His voice will quicken what He has already placed *within* you. He will bring to your awareness the unique part you are created to play in His redemptive programme.

You too, like Abraham, are called to occupy a *place* and produce a *people* in the world. You are destined to influence lives towards God. The call will demand you to leave mediocrity. The call will draw you towards excellence. There is a divine call on your life. There is a magnificent end in view.

Action Page

What have I discovered?

What must I now do?

What questions do I have?

2
TAKING RESPONSIBILITY

*"So he left the land of the Chaldeans and settled in
Haran. After the death of his father, God sent him
to this land where you are now living."*

(Acts 7:4)

*"The Lord had said to Abram, 'Leave your
country, your people and your
father's household and go to the land
I will show you'."*

(Genesis 12:1)

T he one to whom the high calling of God
comes must assume *total responsibility* for
pursuing the call. On the final analysis, you
will be held accountable for your purpose in
life. Doubtlessly, there will be many associations and interactions along the way, but these
should not distract from the journey towards
destiny. The test of every association is its

contribution to purpose and progress. Wrong associations slow you down and *subtract* from you; right associations urge you on and *add* to you. If you are not adding to others and they are not adding to you, there is little need for the fellowship.

God's instruction to Abraham required a separation from his natural relationships. He had to leave his father's household in order to possess the promises of God. However, when the time came for him to leave, Terah, Abraham's father, was the one who *"took his son Abram, his grandson Lot son of Haran, and his daughter-in-law Sarai, the wife of his son Abram, and together they set out from Ur of the Chaldeans to go to Canaan."* (Genesis 11:31). It was to Abraham that God spoke, but the responsibility for action was seconded to Terah. *"Terah took* his son Abraham."

This may seem like a gesture of honour towards an aged father on Abraham's part. However, the time comes when higher honour has to go to the One who deserves it. Ultimately, fleshly sentiments will not serve the purposes of God. Terah and Abraham set out quite alright, but they did not reach God's preordained destination. *"They set out from Ur of the Chaldeans to go to Canaan, but when they came to Haran, they settled there."*

Purpose can only be fulfilled when obedience is complete. You cannot obey half-way and expect full results. Abraham settled in Haran because he did not take *total responsibility* for his destiny. His arrival at Canaan was delayed for as long as he stayed in Haran. Detours from the path of purpose will always delay the time of arrival at the port of destiny.

When the time comes to give account of one's handling of God's instructions, no excuse will be admissible. It does not matter how tenable the alibi. Poor background, less-than-perfect upbringing, inherent weaknesses, family allegiances, none of these will count as worthy reasons for failing to obey God fully and reach your destination. Every man should *take responsibility* for his life and calling. Every call from God comes with Grace for this level of commitment.

Naturally, Abraham was afraid of the unknown. He took a portion of the known with him as a buffer towards the unknown. But each time, God drew him away from this artificial cushion. He had to leave his father (better still, the father left him through death). He also had to leave Lot, his nephew. Fear will always get in the way of complete obedience. Overcoming this fear was part of his lessons in the school of faith.

When the man with a call is ready to take responsibility for his calling, he will have to face his fears. You cannot *negotiate* with fears; you have to *negate* them. You cannot *compromise* with fear; you have to *conquer* it. If you do not conquer your compromise it will end up conquering you. A certain man of God from Judah learnt this lesson too late (Judges 13).

Haran was a place of prosperity that kept Abraham away from true riches. Distraction always comes in disguise. The enemy of God's best is the good that looks good enough. God will not release the blessings of *tomorrow* to the man who cannot sacrifice his *today*. The man who will give up the high call for low comfort is not worthy of the call.

Abraham also had to *take responsibility* for the future. An understanding of what was at stake provoked action in the right direction. A nation was at stake. A kingdom was on the line. The longer he settled in Haran, the further away the promise of greatness. It is a waste of time to desire a great future if you are not willing to take responsibility for creating or taking steps towards it. You cannot just pray or wish for a great future; you have to *take responsibility* for it.

God did not call Abraham to be a *settler*; He called him to be a *pioneer*. Circumstances, however, had conditioned him to be what he was not destined to be. God had to move him on. He had to deal with Terah, the natural father that stood in the way.

After Terah's 205th birthday, he died in the land of his settlement. And after Terah's death, Abraham experienced progress. Sooner or later, God will remove the things that cause delays on the path of purpose. If the man of purpose does not take responsibility, God will—drastically. *It is futile to cling unto something that is marked for destruction.*

Everything outside the remit of purpose should be considered as nothing compared to the surpassing greatness of one's high calling in God. As long as something or someone is considered more important than purpose, distraction from its pursuit will come easily.

After the death of Terah, Abraham revisited God's original call for his life. He was destined for Canaan and not Haran. He was called to possess an entire region for the coming generation of *sons*, not just a small piece of land for himself and his household of *servants*. This realisation made all the difference. It reconnected him to the paths of destiny. *It also prepared him for the secret of greatness and influence, the secret you are about to discover; an important lesson that would secure his placement in heaven's hall of fame.*

Until you perceive a greater tomorrow than today, you will always long for the good, old yesterday. The secret of progress is to judge your present settlement in the light of God's original mandate. No other examination will give the true picture of things. Comparing your achievements with that of others is not wise. Assuring yourself in the mediocrity of yesterday's success is foolishness. Consult the original plan and *take responsibility* for the call. The future of many depends on the responsibilities you assume today.

Over to you

Have you settled in "Haran" when your destination is "Canaan"? Are you prepared to take responsibility for the call on your life?

Progress is measured in terms of the remaining distance to the original mandate. Do not be deceived by present comfort. Where you are today should not keep you from where you are ordained to be tomorrow. God is interested in your *progress* and not just your *prosperity*. True prosperity will be yours as your make progress towards your purpose.

Action Page

What have I discovered?

What must I now do?

What questions do I have?

3
ADVANCED FAITH

"By faith Abraham, when called to go to a place he would later receive as his inheritance, obeyed and went, even though he did not know where he was going."

(Hebrews 11:8)

"So Abram left, as the Lord had told him and Lot went with him. Abram was
seventy-five years old when he set out from Haran.
He took his wife Sarai, his nephew Lot, all the possessions they had
accumulated and the people they had
acquired in Haran, and they set out for the land of Canaan, and they arrived there."

(Genesis 12:4,5)

Faith may *come* by hearing a word from God, but it most certainly *goes* through perpetual inactivity. Abraham is regarded as a man of faith today because he acted on the word of the Lord that came to him. He left Haran *"as the Lord had told him"* and headed for the Promised Land.

Faith is not revealed in the *knowing* but in the *doing*. Likewise, the blessing and commendation of God does not come to the man who merely *answers* his call, but to the one who qualifies himself through decisive *acts of obedience*. Doing nothing with the word of God is as bad as doing something *against* the word. Both will one day attract rebuke and judgement. Abraham was commended for his faith because he proved himself faithful through action.

You cannot *arrive* at your destination until you *leave* your present location. The steps of the righteous man are ordered of God, not the "standing still" of the righteous. There is a time to stand still and a time to step out. Standing still is not a sign of spirituality when God requires action. Even prayer cannot substitute active obedience. It might actually be a cloak of religiosity concealing fear or rebellion. Abraham was not religious; he was a man of faith.

Faith does not rely on the seen. It cannot be subjected to reason or experiments. It is the substance of hope and the evidence of the invisible. It is more tangible than reality itself, not in a physical sense but in realms beyond the visible; the dimensions of the unseen God, the One who never lies nor repents.

Abraham entrusted his future into the hands of the God who called him. He only had an encounter and a promise. The truth is, he had all he needed. This is advanced faith in action.

Elementary faith strives to believe God *for* material things. Advanced faith *forsakes* material things and believes God for eternal things. Faith may be the substance of "things" hoped for but the *kind* of things hoped for determines the *kind* of faith in action.

Abraham's faith went beyond the ordinary; he abandoned the wealth and prospects of Haran for the promise of Canaan. Later in life, the superiority of his faith was evident in the offering of his son to God. Not only did he *"receive Isaac back from death,"* he also saw a vision of the resurrected Christ. The instruction was a test; the obedience of faith was his response; God's everlasting covenant Blessing was his reward! (see Genesis 22; Hebrews 11:17-19).

No-one ever starts with advanced faith. This kind of faith is the result of consistent obedience. God leads in stages so that faith has room and time to develop in the heart. Every act of obedience does not only prove the authenticity of faith, it also develops faith until it grows to become the God-kind of faith. Great faith does not just happen. It *develops*. Little faith, also, is not accidental. It is *potential* faith that *under-develops*.

Every *instruction* from God is an opportunity to move from faith to faith. The instructed, however, determines the resultant measure: from faith to *more* faith or from faith to *less* faith. Faith is never static. It is either increasing or decreasing.

The instructions of God are the link between calling and achievement. He who loves instruction loves life, for the best of the land is available to those who are willingly obedient. The man who is too big to be instructed does not need God. Though he may not admit it, in his mind he feels bigger than the God who is greater than all things put together.

God knows the end from the beginning; He is more than worthy to direct the called towards destiny. Not only does He *know* the way, He *is* the way. Allow Him, then, to lead the way. Just follow Him by faith and all shall be well.

Abraham followed God not knowing where exactly he was going or the route he was to take. He only had a vision born out of a promise, and a full consciousness of the One who promised. True faith does not fidget when all the steps to destiny seem unknown. Its main concern is to remain in touch and in step with the Lord who holds the roadmap to fulfilment.

It is not necessary to understand every minute detail before embarking on the journey of faith; the ability to hear the voice of the Faithful Guide is more paramount. His word is a lamp that guides each step of the sojourner towards purpose and destiny.

The path of faith is *progressive.* It always leads from seed to harvest; from little to plenty. Inevitably, the need to put fleshly comfort to death will arise, launching the man of faith to higher levels of excellence. Such is the experience of anyone who chooses to walk with God; such is the fate of the man called to possess nations by faith.

Without faith, it is not possible to understand and apply the "secret" of Abraham. Without faith, it is not possible to please God either. God did not communicate *this mystery of success* to Abraham until He was sure that Abraham would embrace and run with it. Great secrets are entrusted only to those who trust God wholeheartedly. God does not have favourites, but He confides in those who are totally abandoned to Him and His cause. Others are not worthy of this level of intimacy.

Advanced faith honours God. Tested faith reveals the depth of love for God. Anyone who proves his passion for righteousness through faith and obedience will be loved and honoured by God.

Over to you

Is your faith growing or withering, advanced or elementary? How are you responding to God's instructions that are coming to you today?

The great cloud of faith-witnesses have set the standards below which you should not fall. There is no short-cut to advanced levels of faith; you must trust God explicitly and practically.

God never leads astray. He knows what is best for you. If God says "leave," you cannot afford to stay. If God says "stay," do not leave. Faith and obedience are closely related, for you cannot obey without faith and you cannot claim to walk in faith unless you obey.

Action Page

What have I discovered?

What must I now do?

What questions do I have?

4
THE SECRET

*"Abraham travelled through the land as far as the
site of the great tree of Moreh at Shechem. At that
time the Canaanites were in the land.*

*The Lord appeared to Abraham and said, 'To your
offspring I will give this land.' So he built an altar
there to the Lord, who had appeared to him.*

*From there he went on toward the hills east of
Bethel and pitched his tent, with Bethel on the
west and Ai on the east. There he built an altar to
the Lord and called on the name of the Lord.*

*Then Abraham set out and continued
toward the Negev."*

(Genesis 12:6-9)

T he *secret* of Abraham is *hidden* in this text
that describes his travels. Such is the nature of
secrets; they are always veiled under the
surface, away from the view of common man.

"It is the glory of God to conceal a matter; to search out a matter is the glory of kings" (Proverbs 25:2). In this chapter, the mystery will finally be uncovered for all who desire wisdom for ruling.

Before this revelation is spelt out, though, there is something else in the life of Abraham that is worthy of note. Recall the sequence we have explored so far: he was *called* by *God* to possess a land and produce a people; he *took total responsibility* for his life and his calling; he stepped out *by faith* and "arrived" at Canaan.

Now, instead of revelling at the success of "arriving" at the Promised Land, Abraham *travelled through the land as far as the site of the great tree of Moreh at Shechem... **and continued toward the Negev.**"* It is one thing for you to "arrive," and another thing for you to "continue" until you fully "occupy." Still without a child of his own, Abraham *continued* to walk the length and breadth of his promise. God had promised him an entire region and a coming generation; he was not going to settle for a little patch in an obscure corner.

Behold the challenge of faith: Abraham believed God for a land that was occupied by

Canaanites. He also believed God for a son when both he and his wife had passed the age of childbearing. This is where the secret begins to emerge. *True faith is ready at all times to lay hold of God's promises no matter the prevailing circumstances.*

Abraham did not just walk the land confessing the promise. He did some *deliberate* things everywhere he went. Wherever Abraham sojourned, you will find him engaging in these strategic acts of wisdom and faith. Are you ready for the *secret* of Abraham? See if you can recognise it in the Scripture below:

> *"So he built an altar there to the Lord, who had appeared to him. From there he went on toward the hills east of Bethel and pitched his tent…"*
> ***(Genesis 12:7,8)***

Yes, *the secret* is hidden in the midst of this verse. However, before it is completely unveiled, one more truth is essential.

Abraham had a great promise from God: *"To your offspring I will give this land; all the peoples on earth will be blessed through you."* Nonetheless, he did not *possess* the promise by mere confession. He did not name and claim it either. Abraham laid hold of the promise of God in his life by doing something *specific* towards it. Everywhere he went, Abraham did this *specific* thing; he engaged in this vital activity.

He actually did *three* things, two of which are contained in the text above. Wherever Abraham went, he *built altars* to God and *pitched his tent*. The significance of these two go beyond questioning.

Abraham, as a matter of priority, will always build an altar to the God who appeared to him. The worship and honour of God was his first concern. *He was not in the land of the Canaanites because he sought greatness for himself; he was in a strange land because God had determined to produce a great nation through him.* He did not walk with God because of what he could get *from* God; his life was totally sold out *to* God and His eternal purpose. Having been redeemed from a background of idolatry and sin, Abraham was consumed with the vision of a new order of righteousness and faith. He considered himself blessed above all men to be God's chosen vessel for bringing this level of blessedness to the world. He had to honour God first. He had to build altars unto God. Whoever honours God in this way will surely be honoured by God. Many seek honour today but miss true honour that only God bestows.

Secondly, Abraham *pitched his tent* wherever he went. He did not *build* a house of bricks; he *pitched* a tent of cloth. This, again, reveals Abraham's readiness to move at God's command. It demonstrates his pioneer spirit and total dependence on God. He was flexible in God's hands and not rigid through over-cautiousness. He had no Plan B to preserve his own interests. *"By faith he made his home in the promised land like a stranger in a foreign country; he lived in tents… for he was looking forward to the city with foundations, whose architect and builder is God"* (Hebrews 11:9,10).

Now, if building *altars* unto God and pitching *tents* for his household are two of the three things Abraham did wherever he went, what is the third activity that Abraham engaged in? What is *the secret of Abraham* that enabled him to *practically* possess the land of the Canaanites according to God's promise? We will have to look at a generation after him for an explicit view of this mystery. We will have to take a snapshot from the life of Isaac, Abraham's son:

"From there he went up to Beersheba.

That night the Lord appeared to him and said, 'I am the God of your father Abraham. Do not be afraid, for I am with you; I will bless you and will increase the number of your descendants for the sake of my servant Abraham.'

*Isaac built an altar **there** and called on the name of the Lord. **There** he pitched his tent, and **there** his servants dug a well."*

(Genesis 26:23-25)

Here is the *secret* of Abraham revealed in the life of his son! *Every where he went in the territory of his promise, Abraham did not only build altars to God and pitch tents, **he also dug wells deep into the ground.*** The concrete altars signified his commitment to *worshipping God*; the movable tents symbolised his commitment to *following God*; and the physical wells activated the promise of *possessing the land for God*.

The significance of digging a well in Abraham's day is far-reaching. Not only did it provide a constant supply of water necessary to sustain human and animal life in the oriental heat, it was also a decisive move to stake a claim to the land upon which the well was dug. If someone dug a well (or took over an existing well), he was making a statement of ownership over the land as well. Inevitably, he would attract the attention of those who may rise to dispute the assertion. It could be taken as an entitlement to *territory* or a call for *war*.

This is serious faith in serious action! Although the Canaanites dwelt in the land, Abraham dug wells because God had promised him the land. Even though he was a foreigner, he boldly occupied the land God had given him by faith. God honoured his faith by protecting him from the natives. Abraham was so conscious of God's presence with him; he was not afraid of potential war that could break out against him.

The Philistines could not withstand the authority and blessedness of Abraham. In fact, Abimelech, king of Gerar, had to restore to Abraham the ownership of a well that his servant had seized from Abraham's servants.

Being a man of vision and wisdom, Abraham did not just regain the well, he affirmed and registered his ownership by oath.

Here is the story:

> *"At that time Abimelech and Phicol the commander of his forces said to Abraham, 'God is with you in everything you do. Now swear to me here before God that you will not deal falsely with me or my children or my descendants. Show to me and the country where you are living as an alien the same kindness I have shown you.'*
>
> *Abraham said, 'I swear it.'*
>
> *Then Abraham complained to Abimelech about a well of water that Abimelech's servants had seized. But Abimelech said, 'I don't know who has done this. You did not tell me, and I heard about it only today.'*
>
> *So Abraham brought sheep and cattle and gave them to Abimelech, and the two made a treaty.*
>
> *Abraham set apart seven ewe lambs from the flock, and Abimelech asked Abraham, 'What is the meaning of these seven ewe lambs you have set apart by themselves?' He replied, 'Accept these seven lambs from my hand as a witness that I dug this well.'*

> *So that place was called Beersheba,*
> *because the two men swore an oath there."*
> *(Genesis 21:22-30)*

Abraham affirmed his right to the well and thus the land. He put his roots into the ground for the coming generations. He did not just hope for a manifestation of the promise of God; he obtained the promise of possession by digging and owning wells.

So much is yet to be written about this secret of Abraham. So much will yet be disclosed. If anyone will achieve greatness and fulfil his purpose in life, let him discover his "land of promise" and become a digger of wells, even in the presence of enemies. Well-diggers do not end up as crumb-beggars. Well-diggers glorify God by possessing the land of their promise and extending the rule of God in the earth.

Over to you

Have you discovered the secret of Abraham yet? Are you ready to do all you need to do to practically possess the land God promised?

Your faith in God must translate into this specific act of wisdom: *well-digging*. God will bless the works of your hands and not just the confessions of your faith. After *confession*, you must be ready for *possession*. The only way to possess your promised land is to dig wells deep into the ground.

If you do not become a well-digger, the prophecies over your life will not materialise. You must learn to fight the good fight of faith with the promises you have received from God. The longevity of your influence in life is linked to the physical activity of well-digging. Every well-digger will leave a legacy for coming generations. If you have truly discovered the secret, decide to step out of your comfort zones and put it to good use.

Action Page

What have I discovered?

What must I now do?

What questions do I have?

5
YOUR MANDATE

*"Then God said, 'Let us make man in our image,
in our likeness, and let them rule over the fish of
the sea and the birds of the air, over the livestock,
over all the earth, and over all the creatures that
move along the ground.*

*So God created man in his own image, in the
image of God he created him; male and female he
created them.*

*God blessed them and said to them, 'Be fruitful
and increase in number; fill the earth and subdue
it. Rule over the fish of the sea and the birds of the
air and over every living creature that moves on
the ground.'"*

(Genesis 1:26-28)

E very man recreated in Christ is a bearer of
God's image, and every man created in God's
image has a divine mandate to possess a *land*
and produce a *people* for God. Like Abraham,

the parameters of this *high calling* must be discovered in the Creator and not determined by circumstance. Anyone who chooses to *take responsibility* for the fulfilment of his mandate will not only step out in *faith* but must also understand and apply *the secret of Abraham*. Such a person must become *a significant well-digger*.

Well-diggers are people who have discovered the land of their promise and committed every resource in their disposal to possess it for God's glory. It is not enough to dream about greatness. You cannot confess your way to prosperity. After dreams and confession, you must roll up your sleeves and dig your well. If you do not dig your well, the essential commodity for life will not flow your way. If you do not dig your well, you cannot claim the land for God. If you do not dig your well, any influence you have among men will not last. If you do not dig your well, generations after you will lack supply.

The riches of the earth are buried under its crust. The over-abundant resources that can sustain the six billion people in the world and their coming generations do not lie on the surface. You cannot *wish* them out. You cannot even just *pray* them out. You must *dig* them out.

Likewise, the seeds of greatness with which everyone created in God's image can subdue the earth are locked up in the deep recesses of man's being. They will remain untapped for ages until they are dug up and cultivated. After Abraham prayed on the altars he built for God, he dug wells in the ground God gave to him.

Many are waiting for the wealth of the wicked to be transferred to them. The wise among men are locating the land of their calling and digging wells to retrieve the wealth. They are exercising advanced faith and staking a claim to their God-given land. Life has nothing to offer those who are not ready to engage it. Even God cannot bless the idle soul. If any man would not dig, let him not eat. Most certainly, such a man will not rule. *Only well-diggers rule the earth.*

Well-digging is not a task for the lazy. Its resulting influence is not their honour either.

You cannot rule in the earth until you have claimed some land through well-digging. If you do not subdue your land, you will be subdued by thorns and thistles.

With every God-given purpose there is a God-backed promise. However, the promise is only activated when purpose is pursued with understanding and tenacity.

"The purposes of a man's heart are deep waters,
but a man of understanding
[digs] them out."

(Proverb's 20:5 Author's application)

The understanding you need to realise purpose is *the secret of Abraham*. The key to greatness and influence is found in your commitment to becoming a well-digger. If you have discovered your land of promise, your unique call from God, now activate your understanding of the secret and possess your land through faith and perseverance. Draw out the riches in your land and become a blessing to the generations of men around you.

Remember, Abraham was blessed because God blessed him. Abraham was blessed so he can *be* a blessing. Abraham realised the blessing through obedience, faith and well-digging. You cannot sufficiently bless your world without owning a couple of wells.

All Abraham did was for the furtherance of God's eternal purpose. *He did not dig wells just to provide water for his household; he dug wells to possess the land for God; water flowed as a permanent, additional blessing.* (If he wanted water just for survival, he could have dug wells and remained in Haran). Jesus taught His own the same secret; He taught His disciples to seek *first* the advancement of God's kingdom and its righteousness, and every other necessity of life would be added unto (Matthew 6:33).

The Kingdom does not advance through preaching alone; it also advances through well-digging. The dominion of the King will only extend as far as the wells dug by His servants. Therefore, the great commission Christ handed to his church translates into, *"Go into all the world and dig wells that will bless all men."* This is not only valid; it is urgent. God is in need of well-diggers who will advance His righteous Kingdom by force!

Abraham became a ruler under God, a man

under authority. He also became God's close friend. All this and more because he obeyed God and became a well-digger. It was not an easy path. There was much to learn. There were mistakes and heartaches. There was much Grace and mercy too. Abraham got there at the end, and because he arrived, his seed, the Christ, also arrived.

With this realisation, the journey to becoming a well-digger starts from here. Continuing on this path promises a wealth of opportunities for learning and growing. A true well-digger is open to insight and wisdom. With all your getting, get understanding. Let us embark on this adventure together and make our world a better place.

Over to you

Have you discovered your land of promise? Will you commit your entire life and resources to becoming a well-digger?

Everyone called of God has a *land* to possess and a *people* to produce. The righteous kingdom of God will only extend as far as the "wells" dug by His children. God expects the offspring of Abraham to claim every sector of human existence; He has mandated us to *"fill the earth and subdue it."* Politics, economics, technology, entertainment, sports, the arts, education, social and spiritual sectors; these and other "lands" are to be claimed through purposeful well-digging.

The survival and salvation of a generation of people hinges on you becoming *all* God has ordained for you to be. Life is too short to be wasted on frivolities. Your mandate is too great to be ignored.

Look to Abraham! When God called him he was but one, but with the blessing of God and his commitment to well-digging, he became many. This is *your* story too as you continue in this journey of discovery.

Action Page

What have I discovered?

What must I now do?

What questions do I have?

Join the Well-digger community!

Www.facebook.com/WellDiggerCommunity

**GET ALL THE
WELL-DIGGER BOOKS!**

The Secret of Abraham

The Wells of Isaac

The Destiny of Jacob

The Greatest Well-Digger in the World

*"I am delighted that Tokunbo Emmanuel has
developed this thought-provoking series."*

- Dr. Hugh Osgood

Other books by
Tokunbo Emmanuel

The Shift of A Lifetime

The Mandate of Paul

Faith Clinic Revival

Run, Church Run!

Ultimate Destiny

The Charismatic Agenda

A Scribe's Inspiration

Rediscovering God

Revival in the Desert

Selah Verses

Sharing the Word of God

The Glory of Young Men

31 Nuggets of Inspiration

SOPHOS SB BOOKS

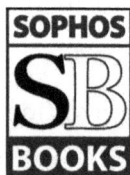

Raising the voice of wisdom!

www.ingramcontent.com/pod-product-compliance
Lightning Source LLC
Chambersburg PA
CBHW060715030426
42337CB00017B/2879